The Conference of Baghdad's Ulema

Translated by
Taher Al-Shemaly

Published by Left of Brain Books

Copyright © 2023 Left of Brain Books

ISBN 978-1-396-32600-4

First Edition

All rights reserved. No part of this publication may be reproduced, distributed, or transmitted in any form or by any means, including photocopying, recording, or other electronic or mechanical methods, without the prior written permission of the publisher, except in the case of brief quotations permitted by copyright law. Left of Brain Books is a division of Left Of Brain Onboarding Pty Ltd.

PUBLISHER'S PREFACE

About the Book

Translation of Mu'tamar 'Ulama' Baghdad.

CONTENTS

PUBLISHER'S PREFACE
    TRANSLATOR'S WORD 1
    THE CONFERENCE OF BAGHDAD'S ULEMA 3

TRANSLATOR'S WORD

THIS is a humble translation for the famous story of "Mu'tamar `Ulamá' Baghdád" which occurred at the time of the Seljuk king Malikshah I (Maliksháh Seljuqi), the son of the Seljuk king Alp Arsalan. Along in this story, the minister or Vizier as was he called, Nizam Al-Mulk, was the minister of Malikshah I and helped him to organize this event. Both of them, the king and the minister were assassinated in the same year of 1092 AD (around 485 AH in Islamic calendar). For more information about the Vizier and the king and also this story, you can refer to wikipedia.

It is interesting to see that the entry in wikipedia contains 3 versions for the story of the assassination of the vizier and the king, and the last version is linked to this story which you are about to see its translation.

Before proceeding in reading, it is better to see some terms:

Ulema: it is used to denote religious scholars who gained a deep insight into religion and its teachings and laws. In modern language Ulema can have the same concept of "Scientists." For this reason I will use the word "Ulema" to denote religious scholars and nothing else.

Ben: A term means "the son of." It was mainly used in old names and still used in some countries to tell the full name of someone.

Pronunciations:

" ' " : Simply, a glottal stop.
" ` " : A hard glottal stop. Like the above but voiced.
Á: Long vowel like in "car" or "father."
Gh: Like french "R" sound.
Kh: Like "CH" in "Bach" or "Loch."
Ð,ð: Like "TH" in "there"
[...]: These brackets to add my own comments.
(PUH): Peace Upon Him. It is an expression used by Muslims for every holy person like the prophet or Jesus or the Household of prophet Mohammed.
(PUT): Peace Upon Them
X:Y : denotes a phrase from Quran. X is the number or order of the chapter, and Y is the number of the phrase.

Translator: Taher Al-Shemaly (TJ)
Kuwait
February, 2007

THE CONFERENCE OF BAGHDAD'S ULEMA

In the name of Allah, the Beneficent, the Merciful

THANKS be to God alone and peace be upon him he who was sent as a mercy for the worlds, Mohammed the arabic prophet and upon his Household, the purified and upon his true followers.

And after that: This is the book of (The conference of the Ulema of Baghdad) that was held between the Sunnis and Shiites that were gathered by the great king (Maliksháh Seljuqi) under the supervision of the great scholar and vizier (Nizam Al-Mulk), and the story was like this:

The king was not an extremist and a blind man, who follow the ancestors with blindness and racism, but he was a young man with an open mind who loves wisdom and Ulema and in the same time he used to like entertainment and hunting.

His Minister (Vizier) was a virtuous wise man who did not indulge in life, with a strong will and liked the goodness and its people, always investigates after the truth, and liked the Household of the prophet so much, and he established the Nizamiyyah school -in Baghdad- and he made for the people of science (wisdom) monthly salaries, and used to be kind over the poor and the needy.

Once upon a time, a great scholar named (Al-Husayn ben Ali Al-`Alawi) entered before the Malikshah and he was one of the greatest Shiites Ulema. When the scholar got out from the court of the king some of the attendance mocked at him, so the king said: why did you mock at him? The man said: Don't you know O king that he is one of the disbelievers that God spread his wrath and damnation over them? The king said -surprised-: and why is that? isn't he a muslim? The man said: no, he is a shiite! The king said then: and what is the meaning of Shiite? aren't shiites one part of muslims' creeds? The man said: no, they don't recognize Abu-Bakr and `Umar and `Uthmán as caliphs, the king then said: and is there a muslim that do not recognize those three as caliphs? The man said: yes, these are the shiites, the king then said: if they don't recognize those three companions of the prophet as caliphs then why do people call them muslims? The man said: that's why I said they are disbelievers.... The king then thought about it for a moment and then said: we should call the vizier Nizam Al-Mulk to see the situation.

The king called Nizam Al-Mulk and asked him about the shiites: are they muslims? Nizam Al-Mulk said: Sunnis differed in that, some of them said that they are muslims because they -the shiites- testify: there is no other god save but Allah, and Mohammed is the prophet of Allah and they pray and fast (in Ramadan), and some of them say that they are disbelievers.

The king said: and how many are they? Nizam Al-Mulk said: I can't count them precisely but they make up almost half of the muslims. The king said: is half of the muslims are all disbelievers? The vizier said: some scholars claim that they are disbelievers but I don't. The king said: then can you O vizier call the scholars of shiites and sunnis to elaborate this matter? The vizier said: this is a difficult task and I'm afraid over the king and the kingdom! The king said: why? The vizier said: because the case of shiites and sunnis is not a simple case, but it is a case of truth and falsehood and many bloodshed ran for this matter and libraries were burnt and women were taken captives and there were many books that were made and wars were started for this matter!!

The young king was surprised for this weird case, then he thought for a moment and said: O vizier, you know that God gave us the wide kingdom and the mighty army so we must thank God for this gift and our thank should be in the form of investigating about the truth and guide the astraying person to the rightful path, and one of these two creeds must be rightful and the other must be wrong, so we must know the truth and follow it and know the wrong path and leave it, so if you - O vizier - prepared such a conference with the attendance of the shiites and sunnis ulema along with the generals and the writers and the rest of the heads of the state, so if we found out that the truth is with sunnis we should then force the shiites to get into that creed by force.

The vizier said: and if the shiites refused to get into the creed of sunnis then what shall you do? The young king said: we kill them! The vizier said: is it possible to kill half of the muslims? The king said: then what is the cure and the solution for this? The vizier said: it is to leave this matter.

The conversation finished between the king and his wise minister, but he remained that night with a busy mind and worried and didn't sleep until next morning, for how come he can't find a solution for this problem. And in the early morning he called Nizam Al-Mulk and said to him: we shall call upon the ulema of the both creeds and we shall see from the arguments and conversations which one is true, and if the truth was with the sunnis then we shall invite the shiites by the wisdom and the good advice and attracted them with money and fortune like how the prophet (PUH) used to do with non Muslims, and in that way we shall be able to serve Islam and muslims. Then said the vizier: your opinion is good, but I'm afraid of this conference! The king said: why the fear? The vizier said: because I'm afraid the shiites will win over the sunnis and their clues will rule over us and people will fall in doubt! The king said: is that possible? The vizier said: yes, because shiites obvious clues from Quran and the Sunna [Sunna means the acts of the prophet that were reported by his companions and followers] that their creed is correct and true! But the king was not convinced by such an answer from his minister (Nizam Al-Mulk) and said to him:

It is a must to bring the ulema from both creeds to discover the truth and make it distinct from falsehood. Then the vizier asked for a time limit of month to prepare the matter, but the young king refused that... and finally it was decided that the time limit should be of fifteen days.

In these days, the vizier (Nizam Al-Mulk) gathered ten men from the greatest sunni ulema that are dependable for history and laws and hadith [hadith: reported speech of the prophet] and the basics and arguing, and brought as well ten of the greatest shiites ulema, and that was in the month of Sha`bán [Sha`bán: 8th month of islamic calendar] in the Nizamiyyah school in Baghdad, and the conference was held upon these conditions:

First: The research should go on from morning until evening with exception to the time of prayers, food and break.

Second: The arguments should depend on assured resources and dependable books and not on what is heard and rumors.

Third: The arguments that go on in this conference shall be recorded.

And on the assigned day, the king sat down and his vizier and his generals and the sunni ulema sat on his right and the shiites ulema sat on his left, and the vizier made the opening for the conference (by saying): In the name of Allah, the Beneficent, the Merciful and peace be upon Mohammed and his Household and his companions, then he said: the argument should be just and asking for the truth should be the goal of everyone and none of the companions of the prophet (PUH) should be insulted.

Said the great scholar of the sunnis (and his title was Al-`Abbási): I can't argue with a creed that make all the companions as disbelievers.

Said the great scholar of the shiites (and his title was Al-`Alawi and his name was Al-Husayn ben Ali): and who are they who make the companions as disbelievers?

`Abbási: you shiites make all the companions as disbelievers.

`Alawi: this talk of you is against the reality. Is not Ali ben Abi Tálib (PUH) and Al-`Abbás and Salmán and Ibn `Abbás and Al-Maqdád and Abu-Ðar and others are all of the companions, so do we shiites make those companions as disbelievers?

`Abbási: I meant by all companions Abu-Bakr and `Umar and `Uthmán and their followers.

`Alawi: you rescinded yourself by yourself, did not the people of logic say that (the partial positive is against the total negative), so you once say that shiites consider all companions disbelievers and once you say that shiites consider some companions disbelievers.

And here the vizier wanted to talk but the shiite scholar didn't give him the chance to do so and said: O great vizier, no one has the right to talk unless we are unable to answer, otherwise it would be a mix up in the research and astraying the argument from its path without any results.

Then the shiite scholar said: I make it clear to you O `Abbási that your claim that shiites consider all the companions disbelievers is an apparent lie.

`Abbási couldn't answer and his face turned red and then he said: leave that and tell me, do you shiites insult Abu-Bakr and `Umar and `Uthmán?

`Alawi: some shiites insult them and some others do not.

`Abbási: and you, `Alawi, in which side are you?

`Alawi: I don't insult, but my opinion that those who insult have their point, and their insults to these three is not a crime and not a disbelief or a heresy and it is not one of the small sins.

`Abbási: did you hear O king what this mean is saying?

`Alawi: O `Abbási, directing the speech to the king is astraying, and the king brought us here to talk about the clues and proves and not to judge by the force and the weapon.

The king: it is true what `Alawi is saying, what is your answer O `Abbási?

`Abbási: it is obvious that he who curses the companions is a disbeliever.

`Alawi: it is obvious for you and not me. What is the clue that everyone who curses the companions after investigating and knowing the truth is a disbeliever? Don't you agree that he who is cursed by the prophet deserves to be cursed?

`Abbási: I do.

`Alawi: then the prophet cursed Abu-Bakr and `Umar.

`Abbási: when did he do that? this is an apparent lie against the prophet.

`Alawi: historians of sunnis mentioned that the prophet prepared an army under the command of Usámah and he made in the army Abu-Bakr and `Umar, and he said: God damns he who lags back from the army of Usámah, and then Abu-Bakr and `Uthmán lagged from the army of Usámah, so they were included in the damnation of the prophet, and he who is damned by the prophet can be damned by any muslim.

Then `Abbási looked down and did not say a word.

Then the king said (to his vizier): is it true what `Alawi said?

Vizier: historians did mention that.[1]

`Alawi: And if insulting the companions was a taboo and a disbelief, then why don't you say that Mu`áwiyah ben Abi Sufyán [Muawiyah I, the first ruler of the Umayyad dynasty] that he is a disbeliever and you don't consider him a heretic for

---

[1] in Tabaqát Ibn Sa`ad, the second section, Part 2, page41 and in Táreekh Ibn `Asákir Part 2, page. 391 and Kanz Al-`Ummál Part 5, page 312 and Al-Kámil for Ibn Al-Atheer Part 2, page 129.

cursing imam Ali ben Abi Tálib (PUH) for 40 years and that extended even further to 70 years!?

The king: cut that discussion and talk about another subject.

`Abbási: one of you innovations you shiites that you don't believe in Quran!

`Alawi: it is but one of your own innovation you sunnis, and the clue is that you say that Quran was gathered by `Uthmán, so was the prophet unwise to do what `Uthmán did, so that he didn't gather the Quran until `Uthmán comes and gather it? Then, how come the Quran was not gathered at the time of the prophet and the prophet used to order his followers and companions to read all the Quran and he said: he who reads all of the Quran gets this and that of such rewards, so is it possible that he orders to read all of the Quran if it was not already gathered, and were muslims all astraying until `Uthman came and saved them? [12]

---

[1] The king (to the vizier): is `Alawi true about what sunnis said about `Uthmán gathering Quran?
Vizier: that's what the interpreters and the historians said.
`Alawi: you should know O king that shiites say that the Quran was gathered at the time of the prophet as you see it now, and no single letter was missed nor added to it, but sunnis say that Quran was added to and some of it was dropped and the prophet didn't gather it but it was gathered by `Uthmán when he became a ruler.
[2] historians mention that `Uthmán gathered the holy books and then burnt it - to mock at it - and so did Al-Bukhári mention in his book in the section of virtues of Quran, and Al-Bayhaqi in his book [Al-Sunan] part 2, page 41, and Kanz Al-`Ummál part 1, page 281, and Al-Taháwi in Mashkal Al-Áthár part 3, page 4. And Oh my God, is the burner of the Quran deserves to be a ruler? What crime can be more awful than this? (the publisher)

`Abbási (and he wanted to take the opportunity): did you hear O king? This man doesn't call `Uthmán a caliph, but he calls him a ruler [meaning a ruler like any ruler and not a legal caliph assigned by muslims].

`Alawi: yes, `Uthmán was not a caliph.

The king: why?

`Alawi: because shiites believe that the rule of Abu-Bakr and `Umar and `Uthmán is illegal!

The king (surprised): why?

`Alawi: because `Uthmán became a ruler by the votes of six men designated by `Umar and all of them didn't vote for `Uthmán except of two or three of them, so the legitimacy of `Uthmán depends on `Umar, and `Umar became a ruler by the will of Abu-Bakr, so the legitimacy of `Umar depends on Abu-Bakr, and Abu-Bakr became a ruler depending on the votes a small group by threatening and force, so the legitimacy of Abu-Bakr depends on force and for this `Umar said about him: the agreement of people for Abu-Bakr to be a ruler was something of the age of ignorance [meaning something barbarous from the era before Islam], may God protect muslims against it and if someone did it again then kill him[1] and Abu-Bakr himself used to say: spare me for I'm not the best of you and Ali is the best within you[2] and for this reason shiites believe that the rule of these is illegal in origin.

---

[1] Sawá`iq Al-Muhriqah for Ibn Hijr page. 8. Al-Milal Wal-Nihal for Al-Shahrestáni and others.
[2] this speech was mentioned by Al-Qawshaji, the sunni scholar in his book "Sharh Al-Tajreed."

The king (to the vizier): is it true what `Alawi is saying about the talk of Abu-Bakr and `Uthmán?

Vizier: yes, this is what the historians mentioned!

The king: then why do we respect these three?

Vizier: following the steps of the good ancestors!

`Alawi (to the king): O king, say to the vizier: is truth worthy to be followed or the ancestors? Is not following the ancestors is against the truth as it is included in God's saying (Nay, for they say only: Lo! we found our fathers following a religion, and we are guided by their footprints, 43:22)!?

The king (to `Alawi): if these three are not the successors of the prophet of God then who is the (rightful) successor?

`Alawi: the successor of the prophet is imam Ali ben Abi Tálib.

The king: and why he is a caliph?

`Alawi: because the prophet assigned him to be a caliph after him[1] where he (the prophet PUH) pointed out that he (imam Ali) shall be the caliph many times, and one of these times is when he (PUH) gathered people in a place between Mecca and Medina called "Ghadeer Khum" and then he raised the hand of Ali and said to muslims: he whoever I'm his ruler, then this is Ali

---

[1] sources that mention that the prophet assigned imam Ali ben Abi Tálib as a caliph are so much and some of them are: Táreekh Ibn Jurayr part 2, page 62. Kanz Al-`Ummál part 6, page392. Saheeh Al-Tarmaði and Saheeh Ibn Májah and Musnad Ahmad ben Hanbal and Mustadrak Al-Saheehayn and Tafseer Al-Rázi and Al-Sawá`iq Al-Muhriqah and other of hundreds of dependable books.

his ruler, O God be on the side of he who is on his side and be an enemy to him who becomes his enemy and be helps who helps him and let down who lets him down, and the he (the prophet) got down from the pulpit and said to muslims -who counted as much as 120,000 persons- : greet Ali by the name of the caliph of believers, so muslims came one by one and they said to Ali: peace upon you O prince of believers, and then came Abu-Bakr and `Umar and greeted Ali (PUH) by the name of the prince of believers and `Umar said: peace upon you O prince of believers, Bakhin Bakhin [bakhin bakhin is an expression of congratulating in Arabic] for you O son of Abu Tálib, you became my prince and the prince of every believing man and woman[1]. Then: the rightful caliph after the prophet (PUH) is Ali ben Abi Tálib.

The king (to the vizier): is it true what was mentioned by `Alawi?

Vizier: so it was mentioned by interpreters and historians.

The king: leave this topic and talk about something else.

`Abbási: shiites claim that Quran was edited (changed).

`Alawi: it is so famous among you - O sunnis - that you say that the Quran was edited.

`Abbási: this is a lie.

---

[1] Mentioned by a large number of historians like: Ahmad ben Hanbal in his Musnad part 4, page281. Al-Rázi in his interpretation, and Al-Khateeb Al-Baghdádi in Táreekh Baghdád part 8, page 280, and Ibn Hijr in his book Al-Sawá`iq Al-Muhriqah page107.

`Alawi: didn't you say in your own books that some phrases about the idols were revealed upon the prophet and then these phrases were erased and canceled out of Quran?

The king (to the vizier): is it true what `Alawi is claiming?

Vizier: yes, that is what was mentioned by historians.

The king: then how come we depend on a Quran that was changed?

`Alawi: you should know O king that we don't say such a thing, but this is the claim of sunnis, and thus Quran for us is dependable but for sunnis it is undependable.

`Abbási: some reported speeches (from the prophet) were mentioned by your own ulema and in your books.

`Alawi: first of all these speeches are few, secondly: they are fake and were made up by the enemies of shiites to lower down the reputation of shiites, and thirdly: the reporters of such speeches and their chains are incorrect, and what is mentioned by some ulema is undependable, but our great ulema that we depend on do not say such a thing and never mention that God praised the idols and said (and forbid that He might say such a thing): these are the great idols, from which forgiveness is asked.

The king: leave this topic and talk about something else.

`Alawi: also sunnis say about God what is not appropriate for him.

`Abbási: like what?

`Alawi: like they say: God is a body, and He, like the human being, laughs and cries and He has a hand and a leg and an eye and a private part and will get His leg into the hell in judgment's day, and He will come down from heaven to the earth on a donkey!

`Abbási: and what's wrong with that, and Quran says (And thy Lord shall come, 89:22) and also says (On the day when it He uncovers a leg, 68:42) [the English translation of Quran does not mention the word "leg" but original Quran says the word "leg"] and also (The Hand of Allah is above their hands 48:10), and the Sunna mentioned that God will put His leg into hell!

`Alawi: what was mentioned in Sunna and Hadith is false for us and bunch of lies, because Abu-Hurayrah and his likes lied about the prophet (PUH) and even `Umar banned Abu-Hurayrah from reporting Hadith and restrained him.

The king (to the vizier): is it true that `Umar banned Abu-Hurayrah from reporting Hadith?

Vizier: yes he did as was mentioned by historians.

The king: then how come we depend on the reported speeches of Abu-Hurayrah.

Vizier: because the ulema depended on his reported speeches.

The king: then, ulema must know better than `Umar because `Umar banned Abu-Hurayrah from reporting Hadith because he told the lies about the prophet but the ulema take his fabricated hadith?!

`Abbási: suppose - O `Alawi - that the speeches about God are not true, but what do you do with the quranic phrases?

`Alawi: Quran contains complete phrases and others that are similar and it has the apparent and the hidden, so the apparent complete is worked with, but the similar should be interpreted according to the basics of the language and the figurative speech and antonomasia, otherwise the meaning will not be acceptable by the mind and the law, so for example: if you considered the phrase (And thy Lord shall come, 89:22) by its apparent meaning then you came against the mind and the law, because mind and law say that God is everywhere and there is no place that is without God, and the apparent meaning of the phrase tells that God is a body, and the body occupies a space and a place, and that means if God is in heavens then He is not on earth and if He is on earth, then heavens shall be out of Him, and this is not true neither by mind nor the law.

`Abbási got confused by this rightful logic and was puzzled to answer and then he said: I don't accept this talk, we should take the apparent meaning of the phrases of Quran.

`Alawi: then what do you do with the similar phrases?? Then, you can't take the apparent meaning of the whole Quran, otherwise your friend sheikh Ahmad `Uthmán (and he was one of the sunni ulema and he was blind) who is sitting beside you should be in hell?

`Abbási: why?

`Alawi: because God says (Whoso is blind here will be blind in the Hereafter, and yet further from the road, 17:72), and since sheikh Ahmad is blind now in this life then he shall blind in the Hereafter and yet further from the road, so do you accept that sheikh Ahmad?

Sheikh Ahmad: no, no, what is meant by "blind" in this phrase is the one who is astraying away from the path of truth.

`Alawi: then, it is proved that one cannot work with the apparent meaning of the whole Quran.

Here, the debate was fierce about the apparent meanings of the Quran, and `Alawi gave many clues to `Abbási that made him speechless, until the king said: leave this topic and move to another.

`Alawi: and one of your innovations -you sunnis- about God that you say that God forces the slaves (humans) to make the sins and the taboo and then judge them for it?

`Abbási: that is true, because God say (He whom Allah sendeth astray, 4:88 and others) and also (Allah hath sealed their hearts, 9:93).

`Alawi: about what you said that is it in Quran, the answer to that is: Quran has many figurative language usages that must be explained, so the meaning of "astraying" is that God leaves the wicked person and does not care about him until he goes astraying, and this is like when we say (the government spoiled the people), and that means that the government left the people and did not take care of them , this is first. Secondly, didn't you hear God's saying (Allah, verily, enjoineth not lewdness, 7:28) and also (Lo! We have shown him the way, whether he be grateful or disbelieving, 76:3) also (And guide him to the parting of the mountain ways, 90:10). Thirdly, it is not acceptable logically that God orders people to do the sin and then punish for it, because this is even far away from the habit of the normal people then how come it is something for

God the Exalted and the Just, Exalted He is and Sanctified from what the disbelievers and the unjust say and High Exalted above what they say.

The king: no, no, is it impossible that God forces the human to do the sin and then punish him, this is exactly the wrong, and God is Exalted from being unjust and corrupt (Allah is no oppressor of (His) bondmen), but I don't think that sunnis follow the argument of `Abbási?

Then he asked the vizier and said: do sunnis follow that?

Vizier: yes, this is what is known among the sunnis!

The king: how come they say what is against the logic?

Vizier: they have interpretations and clues.

The king: whatever interpretation and clue is that it is impossible for me to see and accept except of what `Alawi said about that God never forces anyone to do the sin and then punishes for it!

`Alawi: then, sunnis also say that the prophet (PUH) was doubtful about his prophecy.

`Abbási: this is an apparent lie.

`Alawi: don't you say in your own books that the prophet of God said "every time that Gabriel does not come down for me, I think that he got down on Ibn Al-Khattáb [meaning `Umar]," and you should know that there are many holy phrases that points out that God made a covenant with the prophet Mohammed (PUH) for his prophecy?

The king (to the vizier): is it true what `Alawi is saying about this hadith being in the books of sunnis?

Vizier: yes, it is in some books[1].

The king: this is truly a disbelief.

`Alawi: and sunnis also say in their books that the prophet (PUH) used to carry `Á'ishah [one of the prophet's wives] on his shoulders to watch the flute players and drum players, so is that suitable for the situations and the level of the prophet of God?

`Abbási: this is not harmful.

`Alawi: do you do that and you are a normal person, do you carry your wife upon your shoulders to watch the players?

The king: he who was the least shyness and jealousy won't allow such a thing, then how is it with the prophet with all his faith. Is it true that such a thing is there in the books of sunnis?

Vizier: yes, it is in some books!

The king: how come we believe in a prophet that doubts about his prophecy?

`Abbási: this hadith should be interpreted?

`Alawi: does this hadith require an interpretation? Do you know now O king that sunnis believe in such innovations and lies?

`Abbási: what lies do you mean?

---

[1] mentioned by Ibn Abi Al-Hadeed Al-Mu`tazali in Sharh Al-Manhaj, and others

`Alawi: I've explained to you now that you say:

1. God is like human who has a hand and a leg and moves and settles down.

2. Quran had been edited.

3. The prophet does what even normal people never do like carrying `Á'ishah on his shoulders.

4. The prophet was doubtful about his prophecy.

5. Who came to the throne before Ali ben Abi Tálib, used force and the sword to prove themselves and they are not legitimate (to be rulers).

6. Your books tell hadith from Abu-Hurayrah and his likes of liars and such lies.

The king: leave this topic and move to another.

`Alawi: and then, sunnis claim about the prophet (PUH) what is not appropriate even for the normal man!

`Abbási: like what?

`Alawi: like claiming that the phrase (He frowned and turned away, 80:1) [the holy phrases continue and talk about a blind man] was revealed about the prophet!

`Abbási: and what is wrong with that?

`Alawi: it is wrong because God said (And lo! thou art of a tremendous nature, 68:4) [and in my own translation the phrase would be more like: thou art of great manners] and also (We sent thee not save as a mercy for the peoples, 21:107). Is it reasonable that the prophet who is described by God to be of a tremendous nature (manners) and also a mercy for the peoples, is it reasonable that he does such a inhumane thing with the faithful blind man??

The king: it is impossible that such a thing could be done by the messenger of humanity and the prophet of mercy, then `Alawi about whom these phrases were revealed?

`Alawi: the correct hadiths that we have and are reported by the way of the Household of the prophet, them who Quran was revealed in their houses, all these hadiths say that it was revealed about `Uthmán ben `Affán [the third caliph], and that was when Ibn Um Maktoom [who was a blind man] met `Uthmán and `Uthmán turned back at him.

Here, Sayed Jamál Al-Deen (and he is one of the shiite ulema and was in the court) said: an incident happened with me about this phrase and that was when a christian scholar said to me: our prophet Jesus is better than your prophet Mohammed, so I said: why? He said: because your prophet was ill mannered and frowned for the blind men and turns back at them, while Jesus was good mannered and healed the blind and the leper. I said: O christian, you should know that we shiites say this phrase was revealed about `Uthmán ben `Affán and not about the prophet (PUH) and our prophet was good mannered with beautiful manners, and God said about him (And lo! thou art of a tremendous nature, 68:4) and also (We sent thee not save as a mercy for the peoples, 21:107). The christian said: I heard this talk I said to you from a preacher in a mosque in Baghdad!

`Alawi: what is known among us is that some of the ill narrators and those who have no conscious claimed that this story happened with the prophet to clean the record of `Uthmán ben `Affán , so they lied about the prophet just to make their caliphs and rulers like innocents!

The king: leave this topic and talk about another.

`Abbási: shiites deny that the three caliphs were believers, and this is not true, because if they were not then why did the prophet allow them to marry his daughters?

`Alawi: shiites believe that these -three- were not believers in heart and they got into Islam just by the tongue, and the great prophet (PUH) used to accept the Islam of anyone who testifies the two [meaning: testify that God is one and Mohammed is a prophet] even if he was a hypocrite and he used to treat all like muslims, so the relation between them and the prophet was in the way of this logic!

`Abbási: what is your clue that Abu-Bakr was not a faithful?

`Alawi: the apparent clues are a lot, and one of them is: he betrayed the prophet many times like when he disobeyed the prophet and didn't join the army of Usámah, and Quran foretold that he who disobeys the prophet is not a believer, God says (But nay, by thy Lord, they will not believe (in truth) until they make thee judge of what is in dispute between them and find within themselves no dislike of that which thou decidest, and submit with full submission, 4:65). So, Abu-Bakr disobeyed the command of the prophet and went against it so he is included in this holy phrase. Add to that, the prophet (PUH) damned him who lags behind from the army of Usámah and we mentioned before that Abu-Bakr lagged behind from the army of Usámah, so does the prophet damn a believer? Of course: no.

The king: so the argument of `Alawi about him [Abu-Bakr] that he was not a believer!

Vizier: sunnis got interpretations about his lagging.

The king: does interpretation push away what is prohibited? If we opened this door then every criminal shall have the excuse for his crime. So the thief shall say: I've stolen because I'm poor, and the drunk shall say: I've drunk because I have so much troubles, and the adulterer say this and that, and so the whole system will be shaken up and the people will dare more to disobey, no... no... interpretations are not useful for us.

The face of `Abbási turned red and was puzzled, what shall he say, and finally he said hardly: and what is the clue that `Umar was not a believer?

`Alawi: there are many clues, one of them is that he himself declared that he is not faithful!

`Abbási: when?

`Alawi: when he said (I was not doubtful about the prophecy of Mohammed like I was at the day of Hudaybiyyah) [Hudaybiyyah, a place in Saudi Arabia at which the prophet made a truce with the idolaters of Mecca] and his talk denotes that he was always doubtful about the prophecy of our prophet, and his doubt at the day of Hudaybiyyah was even deeper, so tell me -O `Abbási- by God, he who is doubtful about the prophecy of Mohammed (PUH) is considered a believer?

`Abbási went silent and looked down.

The king (to the vizier): is `Alawi right about what `Umar said?

Vizier: this is what was said by the narrators!

The king: amazing... so amazing... I used to consider `Umar one of first muslims, and used to consider his faith to be a unique one and now I see that his faith was mixed with doubt!

`Abbási: hold on O king and stay on your creed, and don't be tricked by this lying `Alawi.

The king turned his face away from `Abbási and said with anger: the vizier

Nizam Al-Mulk say that `Alawi is true about his argument, and the talk of `Umar is mentioned in the books and this idiot - `Abbási- say that he is a liar, isn't that exactly what is meant by stubbornness?

The court went under a deep silence, because the king was greatly annoyed by what `Abbási said... and `Abbási looked down with the rest of the sunni ulema... and the vizier went silent... and `Alawi remained looking up at the face of the king to see the result.

They were hard moments for `Abbási, and he wished that earth would split and swallow him down, or the angel of death would come down and take his soul out for the embarrassment and the critical situation, for the falsehood of his creed showed up in front of the king and the vizier and the rest of ulema and generals... but what shall he do? The king brought him here to ask and answer and to know truth from the falsehood, and for this, he gathered his power and looked up and said: and how do you say O `Alawi that `Uthmán was not a believer at heart while the prophet made him marry both his daughters Ruqayyah and

Um-Kalthoom? [notice that recent studies point out that probably the prophet never hard these daughters but they are merely made up names].

`Alawi: the clues about his ill faith and it is enough to say that muslims -including the companions- gathered and killed him, and you say that the prophet said: my nation never gathers upon a wrong matter, so do muslims -including the companions- gather to kill a believer? And `Á'ishah used to compare him with jews and ordered to kill him and said: kill Na`thal -a name of a jew man- because he is a disbeliever, kill Na`thal may God kill him[1], damned he may be. Also, `Uthmán beat `Abdullah ben Mas`ood the great companion until he got hernia and made him remain in bed until he died. Also, he deported Abu-Ðar Al-Ghifári, that great companion that the prophet said about him (no green cover made a shade for nor the desert carried someone that has a truthful tongue more than Abu-Ðar), and he deported him away from Medina to Shám [Shám: lands of Syria and the surroundings] for once or twice and then to Al-Rabaðah, and it is a dry land between Mecca and Medina - until Abu-Ðar died out of hunger and thirst - at the time that `Uthmán was spreading the treasury of muslims over his relatives of umayyads and marwanids!

The king (to the vizier): is `Alawi true about what he said?

---

[1] Ibn Abi Al-Hadeed Al-Mu`tazali said in Sharh Nahj Al-Balaghah part 2, page77: everyone who wrote history and made classifications about it mentioned that `Á'ishah was one of the fiercest people over `Uthmán and she got one of the prophet's shirts and made a stand for it in her house and used to say to whoever comes in: this is the shirt of the prophet did not decay and `Uthmán made his own clothes decay.

Vizier: historians mentioned that![1]

The king: how come then muslims claimed him a caliph?

Vizier: by voting.

`Alawi: wait O vizier, don't say what is untrue!

The king: what are you saying O `Alawi?

`Alawi: the vizier made a mistake in his talk, because `Uthmán came to the throne by the will of `Umar and the votes of three hypocrites and they are: Talhah, and Sa`ad ben Abi Waqás and `Abdul-Rahmán ben `Awf, so do these three resemble all muslims? And then, historians mention that these who voted, changed their minds about `Uthmán when they saw his tyranny and his disrespect for the companions of the prophet (PUH) and how he asked for advice about the matters of muslims from Ka`b Al-Ahbár the jew [the great rabbi] and how he spread the treasury of muslims among the marwanids, so these three started to stir up people to kill `Uthmán!

The king (to the vizier): is it true what `Alawi just said?

---

[1] Historians mentioned that `Uthmán gave `Abdullah ben Khálid ben Usayd 400,000 dirham, and Al-Hakam ben Al-`Ás -who was deported by the prophet- 100,000 dirham, and gave the land of Fadak to Marwán ben Al-Hakam, and the land of Fadak was for Fatima [the daughter of the prophet] but it was taken by force by Abu-Bakr and `Umar, and then it was given by `Uthmán to Marwán - and also gave `Abdullah ben Ubay the fifth of Africa in the same day that he gave Marwán 100,000 dirham, and all of that was out of the treasury of muslims. Get back to the details in Sharh Nahj Al-Balaghah for Ibn Abi Al-Hadeed Al-Mu`tazali part 1, to find the details. (the publisher)

Vizier: yes, this is what historians mentioned!

The king: then how come you said he ruled by voting?

Vizier: I meant the votes of these three!

The king: and is choosing three men makes the voting correct?

Vizier: these three were testified to be in paradise by the prophet (PUH)!

`Alawi: wait O vizier, don't say what is untrue, the hadith of the (10 people in paradise) is just a lie about the prophet (PUH)!

`Abbási: how come you say it is a lie and assured narrators mentioned this?

`Alawi: there are lot of clues that tell this hadith is a lie and not true, and I shall mention three of them:

First: how come the prophet testifies that someone is in paradise for someone who hurt him and that is Talhah? Some historians and interpreters mentioned that Talhah said: if Mohammed died we shall marry his wives after him -or- I shall marry `Á'ishah, so the prophet was hurt a lot by the talk of Talhah and God revealed the phrase (And it is not for you to cause annoyance to the messenger of Allah, nor that ye should ever marry his wives after him. Lo! that in Allah's sight would be an enormity, 33:53).

Second: Talhah and Al-Zubayr fought against imam Ali ben Abi Tálib (PUH) and the prophet (PUH) said about Ali (O Ali, your war is my war and your peace is my peace)¹, and also said (he who obeyed Ali had obeyed me and he who disobeyed Ali had disobeyed me)², and also said (Ali is with the Quran and the Quran is with Ali never separated until they come back to me at the Fountain) [the Fountain, a place at the time of the judgment day when the prophet of Muhammad is believed to wait for his followers]³, and also said (Ali is with the truth and the truth is with Ali ... and it revolves with him wherever he goes)⁴, so, is the one who fights against the prophet and disobeyed him shall be in paradise? Is the fighter against the truth and Quran is considered a believer?

Third: Talhah and Zubayr prepared the way to kill `Uthmán, so is it possible that `Uthmán and Talhah and Zubayr are all in paradise and they fought against each other, and the prophet (PUH) said (the killer and the killed are all in hell)??

The king (surprised): is all what `Alawi said true? and here the vizier went silent and didn't say a thing, and `Abbási went silent and didn't say a thing. What shall they say? Would they say the truth? Does Satan allow them to admit the truth? Does the soul who orders with badness allow itself to be under the truth? Do you think admitting the truth is an easy task?

---

[1] mentioned by Al-Khateeb Al-Khawárizmi in the book of Al-Manáqib page76, and mentioned by Ibn Hasnaweh and mentioned by Al-Qandoozi in his book Yanabee` Al-Mawaddah page130, and lot of other great ulema of sunnis.

[2] Kanz Al-`Ummál Hadith #1213, and others.

[3] Kanz Al-`Ummál Hadith # 1152, and Al-Sawá`iq page75 and Mustadrak Al-Hákim page124.

[4] Táreekh Baghdád part 14, page321, and Al-Háfidh Al-Haythami in Majma` Al-Zawá'id part 7, page236, and Ibn Qutaybah in Al-Imámah Wal-Siyásah part 1, page68 and Mustadrak Al-Hákim part 3, page125, and Jámi` Al-Tarmaði part 2, page213 and others. (publisher)

No... it is a hard thing, because it requires neglecting racism of the ignorance age and going against the will of the soul, and the people usually go after the soul and the falsehood except of the faithful and how few are they!

`Alawi torn out the curtain of silence and said: O king, the vizier and `Abbási and all of these ulema know the truth in my speech and talk and how true is my argument, and if they denied this, then in Baghdad there are ulema that testify for my argument to be true, and in the stores of this school there are books that testify that my argument is true, and resources that announce apparently how truthful is my argument is... so if they admitted that my argument is true, then this is what is required, otherwise I'm ready now to bring you the books and the resources and the witnesses!

The king (to the vizier): is the talk of `Alawi about the truthfulness of his argument in books and resources true?

Vizier: yes.

The king: why were you silent in the beginning then?

Vizier: because I hate to stab in the reputation of the companions of the prophet (PUH)!

`Alawi: amazing! you hate that and God with His prophet (PUH) did not hate that when God identified some of the companions as "hypocrites" and He ordered His prophet to fight them like he fights against the disbelievers, and the prophet himself damned some of his companions!

Vizier: didn't you hear O `Alawi that ulema said: all the prophet's companions are equal?

`Alawi: I heard that, and I know it is a lie, because how come all of them are equal and God damned some of them and the prophet damned some of them and some of them damned each other and fought against each other and some of them cursed each other and some of them killed each other?

Here, `Abbási found the door closed in his face, so he came through some other door and said: O king, ask this `Alawi, if the caliphs were not believers then how come muslims chose them to be so and followed them?

`Alawi: first, not all muslims followed them and only sunnis did so. Second, those who believed in their ruling are divided into two: an ignorant and a stubborn, as for the ignorant one he does not know their realities but imagine them as good kind and faithful people, and as for the stubborn one, clues and proves are not useful with him as long he insisted on being stubborn and arguing

God said (Whether thou warn them or thou warn them not, it is alike for them, for they believe not, 36:10)!

Third: those who chose these to be caliphs made a mistake like how christians made a mistake when they said (the Messiah is the son of God) and like how jews made a mistake when they said (`Uzair [Ezra] is the son of God), so the human should obey God and the prophet and follow the truth, not follow the people with their falsehood and wrong, and God says (Obey Allah and obey the messenger, 5:92).

The king: leave this topic and talk about something else.

`Alawi: and one of the mistakes of the sunnis and their innovations that they didn't follow Ali ben Abi Tálib (PUH) and followed others.

`Abbási: and why is that?

`Alawi: because Ali ben Abi Tálib (PUH) was appointed by the prophet (PUH) and the other three were not; and he (`Alawi) continued: O king, if you appointed someone to succeed you, should the ministers and the members of the government follow you? or they have the right to isolate your successor and place someone else in his place?

The king: no but they should follow my successor who was appointed by me, and follow him and obey my command about him.

`Alawi: this is what shiites did, they followed the successor of the prophet (PUH) who was appointed by the prophet (PUH) by a command from God the Exalted, and that is Ali ben Abi Tálib, and they (shiites) left others.

`Abbási: but Ali ben Abi Tálib was not appropriate to be a caliph, because he was young while Abu-Bakr was older, and Ali ben Abi Tálib killed the bravest arabs, so arabs wouldn't accept him, while Abu-Bakr was not like that!

`Alawi: did you hear O king? `Abbási is saying that people know more than God and His prophet in appointing the best, because he doesn't follow what was appointed by God and His prophet (PUH) about Ali ben Abi Tálib, but follows what some people say about Abu-Bakr. Like if God does not know what is best, until some ignorant people come and choose the best? Did not God say (And it becometh not a believing man or a believing woman, when Allah and His messenger have decided an affair (for them), that they should (after that) claim any say in their affair; and whoso is rebellious to Allah and His messenger, he verily goeth astray in error manifest, 33:36)?

Did not God say (O ye who believe! Obey Allah, and the messenger when He calleth you to that which quickeneth you, 8:24)?

`Abbási: no I didn't say that people know better than God and His prophet (PUH).

`Alawi: then your argument has no meaning, if God and the prophet appointed one person for the caliphate and to be an imam, so you should follow it, either you are satisfied with it or not!

`Abbási: but the qualifications in Ali ben Abi Tálib were few.

`Alawi: first, the meaning of your argument is that God did not know who is Ali ben Abi Tálib exactly, so he didn't know that his qualifications were few and for this He appointed him as a caliph and this is obvious disbelief. Secondly, in reality, the qualifications to be a caliph and an imam were abundant in Ali ben Abi Tálib, while others did not have such qualifications!

`Abbási: and what are these qualifications -for example-?

`Alawi: his qualifications are so much, and first of all is that he was appointed by God and His prophet (PUH). Secondly, he was the most wise of all the companions, and thus the prophet... said (Ali is the most just) and `Umar ben Al-Khattáb said (Ali is the most just among us)[1], and the prophet said (I am the city of knowledge and Ali is its gate, whoever wanted the city shall enter from its gate) [2], and he himself (PUH) said (the prophet taught me one thousand sections of knowledge, from each section I get one thousand sections opened)[3], and obviously the wise one is advanced over the ignorant, and God says (Are those who know equal with those who know not?, 9:39). Thirdly, he was not in need of others, and others were in need of him, did not Abu-Bakr say (spare me for I'm not the best of you and Ali is the best within you)? Did not `Umar say in more than 70 occasions (if it wasn't for Ali,...

`Umar surely was doomed) [4] and (may God never leave me for a problem that you are not in it O Abul-Hasan [meaning imam Ali]) [5] and also (no one shall judge in the mosque while Ali is present)? Fourthly, Ali ben Abi Tálib never disobeyed God and never worshipped something else other than God, and never prostrated for an idol in his life, and these three disobeyed God and worshipped someone other than God and worshipped idols

---

[1] Saheeh Al-Bukhári about the interpretation of God's saying (Nothing of our revelation (even a single verse) do we abrogate or cause be forgotten... 2:106), and Tabaqát Ibn Sa`d part 6, page102, and Al-Istee`áb part 1, page8, and part 2, page461, and Hilyat Al-Awliyá' part 1, page65, and lot of others.

[2] Mustadrak Al-Hákim part 3, page126, Táreekh Baghdád part 4, page348, and Asad Al-Ghábah part 4, page22, Kanz Al-`Ummál part 6, page152, and Tahðeeb Al-Tahðeeb for Ibn Hijr part 6, page 320, and others.

[3] Nahj Al-Balaghah

[4] Al-Hákim fi Al-Mustadrak, Kitáb Al-Salát part 1, page358, Al-Istee`áb part 3, page39, and Manáqib Al-Khawárizmi page48, and Taðkirat Al-Sibt page87, and Tafseer Al-Naysáboori in the interpretation of Surat Al-Ahqáf [that is Quran, chapter 46] and others.

[5] Taðkirat Al-Sibt page87, Manáqib Al-Khawárizmi page60, and Faydhul-Qadeer part 4, page357.

and God said (My covenant includeth not wrong-doers, 2:124), and obviously, he who disobeys (God) is a wrong-doer, so he is not qualified to take the covenant of God, that is, the prophecy or being caliph. Fifthly: Ali ben Abi Tálib was one of right mind and an open mind and a right opinion that originated from Islam, while others had opinions originating from Satan, and so Abu-Bakr said (I have a satan that wears me) and `Umar disobeyed the prophet in many occasions, and `Uthmán was of weak opinion and affected by his bad companions like: Al-Wazagh ben

Al-Wazagh [wazagh: an arabic name for some type of lizards] who was damned by the prophet and he damned his descendants - except of the believers and how few are they - (Marwán ben Al-Hakam) and also Ka`b Al-Ahbár the jew and others.

The king: is it true that Abu-Bakr said (I have a satan that wears me)?

Vizier: this is found in the books of history! [1]

The king: and is it true that `Umar disobeyed the prophet?

Vizier: we shall ask `Alawi what he means by this?

`Alawi: yes, sunni ulema mentioned in assured books that `Umar disobeyed the prophet in many occasions, like:

1. when the prophet wanted to pray upon `Abdullah ben Ubay, when `Umar replied back the prophet with a harsh answer and

---

[1] Tabaqát In Sa`d part 3, section 1, page129, and Táreekh Ibn Jurayr part 2 page 440, and Al-Imámah Wal-Siyásah for Ibn Qutaybah page6, and others. (the publisher)

the prophet was hurt from that and God says (Those who vex the messenger of Allah, for them there is a painful doom, 9:61).

2. when the prophet (PUH) ordered to separate `Umrat Al-Tamattu` and Hajj Al-Tamattu` [two duties of pilgrimage] and he (PUH) allowed that a man can reach his wife between the both duties, then `Umar refused that and said this hideous sentence (shall we prepare for pilgrimage and our organs are still dropping the semen?) and the prophet answered him: you never believed in it, and by that sentence the prophet (PUH) made him know himself that he is one of those who believe in some and neglect some.

3. about the Mut`ah marriage [Mut`ah marriage is a type of temporal marriage] when he did not believe in it, and when he came to the throne by force he said (2 Mut`as that were at the time of the prophet and now I ban them and punish for them) while God says (And those of whom ye seek content (by marrying them), give unto them their portions as a duty, 4:24) [the English translation doesn't bring the real meaning as in the original Arabic text where the action of Mut`ah is obvious], and interpreters said that it was revealed about allowing Mut`ah marriage, and muslims used to do that until the days of `Umar, and when `Umar banned it, adultery increased among muslims[1], and by doing this `Umar stopped working with one law of God and His prophet (PUH) and made the way open for adultery! and got himself included in the phrases (Whoso judgeth not by that which Allah hath revealed: such are disbelievers...wrong-doers...evil-livers, 5:44,45,47).

---

[1] as reported from imam Ali ben Abi Tálib (PUH) that he said: if it was not for `Umar banning Mut`ah, then no one would commit adultery except of the unblest.

4. in the occasion of Hudaybiyyah as mentioned before. and in some other occasions where `Umar used to refuse the commands of the prophet and hurt him with his harsh words.

The king: truly, I don't also accept the idea of Mut`ah (of women)!

`Alawi: do you admit that it is an islamic law or not?

The king: I don't.

`Alawi: then what's the meaning of the phrase (And those of whom ye seek content (by marrying them), give unto them their portions as a duty, 4:24)? and what is the meaning of `Umar's saying (2 Mut`as..etc)? Does not the saying of `Umar point out that the marriage of Mut`ah was allowed during the time of the prophet, and even at the days of Abu-Bakr, and part of the time of `Umar and then he banned it? Adding to that other clues and they are a lot, O king, `Umar himself used to marriage in Mut`ah and `Abdullah ben Al-Zubayr was born from Mut`ah!

The king: what do you say O vizier?

Vizier: the clue of `Alawi is correct, but since `Umar banned it, we should follow him.

`Alawi: is God and the prophet are better to be followed or `Umar? Hadn't you read, O vizier, God's saying (And whatsoever the messenger giveth you, take it 59:7) and (and obey the messenger, 5:92, and many others), and also (Verily in the messenger of Allah ye have a good example, 33:21) and also the famous hadith (the allowed thing of Mohammed is allowed until the judgment day and the taboo of Mohammed is taboo until the judgment day)?

The king: I believe in all of the laws of Islam, but I don't understand why Mut`ah is allowed, for does any of you desires to give his daughter or his sister to a man, to enjoy with her for one hour, isn't that hideous?

`Alawi: and what do you say about that O king: does someone want to give his daughter or his sister for normal marriage for a man, while he knows that she will be divorced after one hour?

The king: I don't want that.

`Alawi: although sunnis believe that such normal marriage is correct, and the divorce in that case is correct too, and the difference between Mut`ah and normal marriage is that Mut`ah is over when its assigned time is up and the normal marriage is over by divorce, and in other words: Mut`ah marriage is like a contract of renting, and normal marriage is like a contract of ownership, when renting is over by the end of the assigned time and the ownership could be over by selling -for example-! Then, allowing Mut`ah is correct because it is for satisfying one of the needs of the body.

Like how the normal marriage which ends by divorce is correct because it is a way to satisfy one of the needs of the body. Then I shall ask you O king, what do you say about those widows who lost their husbands and none came to marry them, isn't Mut`ah is the only solution for them to protect them from adultery and mischief? Isn't it by Mut`ah that they can get some money for themselves and to take care of their orphans? And what do you say about the young people and the men that their circumstances doesn't allow them to get married, isn't Mut`ah is the only solution for them to get rid of the tremendous sexual force?! And to protect them against mischief? Isn't Mut`ah better than adultery, and sodomy and the secret habit [masturbation]? I think - O king - that every crime of adultery or sodomy or a masturbation that happens between people is because of `Umar, and he shares its badness, because he is the one who banned it! And there are many news that tells how adultery increased among people since `Umar banned Mut`ah! and your saying - O king - that you don't want to ...etc, well, Islam did not force anyone to do so, and did not force you to let your daughter get married for someone that you know he will divorce her after one hour of marriage, beside that, your desire and the desire of people of not wanting this, that is not a base for making something a taboo, because the law of God is fixed and does not change by opinions and desires!

The king (to the vizier): the clue of `Alawi about Mut`ah is strong!

Vizier: but the ulema followed `Umar.

`Alawi: first, the ulema who followed `Umar are the sunni ones only and not all of them, second, the law of God and His prophet is the one to follow or `Umar's? Third, your ulema went against the law of `Umar by themselves.

Vizier: how?

`Alawi: because `Umar said (2 Mut`as that were at the time of the prophet and I ban them: Hajj Al-Tamattu` and Mut`ah marriage), so if the argument of `Umar was right then why didn't your ulema follow his argument in Hajj Al-Tamattu`? While your ulema went against `Umar and said that Hajj Al-Tamattu` is correct, although `Umar banned it! And if the argument of `Umar is false then why did your ulema follow his argument about Mut`ah marriage?

The vizier went silent.

The king (to the attendance): why don't you answer `Alawi?

Then said one of the shiites ulema and his name was sheikh Hasan Qásimi: the problem of `Umar and them who followed him is obvious, thus, these people - O king - have no answer for `Alawi, may God save him.

The king: then leave this topic and talk about something else.

`Abbási: these shiites claim that `Umar has no virtue, and it is enough for him that he made all of these invasions for the islamic state.

`Alawi: we have answers for that: first: rulers and kings invade the land to expand their territories, so is this a virtue? second: if we believed that his invasions were a virtue, but do these invasions excuse him for taking the caliphate by force? And the situation is that the prophet (PUH) did not assign him to be a caliph but gave that position to Ali ben Abi Tálib (PUH)... for if you - O king - assigned a successor for yourself, and then someone came and took that place instead of your assigned successor, and then he made the invasions and did the good deeds, would be satisfied with his invasions or shall you be angry at him, because he took the place of your own successor and isolated your successor without your permission?

The king: I shall be angry at him and his invasions do not wash his crime!

`Alawi: and so did `Umar, he took the place of the caliphate and sat in the place of the prophet without the prophet's permission! third: the invasions of `Umar were wrong and it had a negative effect, because the prophet (PUH) never attacked anyone, but his wars were for defence only, and that's why people liked Islam and got into the religion of God in large numbers because they knew that Islam is a religion of peace, but as for `Umar he attacked the lands and got them into Islam by force and the sword, and for this people hated Islam and claimed that it is the religion of the sword and the force, and not the religion of logic and easiness and that was the cause for the many enemies of Islam, so: the invasions of `Umar corrupted the reputation of Islam and gave a negative reversed effect. And if Abu-Bakr and `Umar and `Uthmán did not take the caliphate for themselves from the true imam, imam Ali (PUH), and if the imam was taking care of the caliphate directly after the prophet, then he would be walking on the steps of the prophet and apply his right methods, and that would be a source for getting more people into Islam, and the expansion of Islam would reach the whole earth! But, there is no might save but by Allah.

Here, `Alawi took a deep breath and moaned from the depth of his heart and hit one hand over the other for his sorrow about Islam and what happened to it after the death of the prophet (PUH) because of taking the caliphate from its rightful owner: imam Ali (PUH).

The king (to `Abbási): what is your answer to `Alawi's talk?

`Abbási: I've never heard such a thing before!

`Alawi: now since you've heard it and knew the truth, leave your caliphs and follow the rightful caliph for the prophet (PUH) Ali ben Abi Tálib (PUH). Then he continued: amazing is your logic O sunnis, you forget the origin and take the branch.

`Abbási: how is that?

`Alawi: because you mention the invasions of `Umar and forget the invasions of Ali (PUH)!

`Abbási: and what are the invasions of Ali ben Abi Tálib?

`Alawi: most of the invasions of the prophet were done by the hand of Ali ben Abi Tálib like Badr and Khaybar and Hunayn and Uhud and Al-Khandaq and others... and if it was not for these invasions (battles) that formed the base for Islam, there wouldn't be `Umar, nor Islam nor a faith, and the clue to that is when the prophet (PUH) said -when Ali went to fight `Amr ben `Abd-Wid at the battle of Khandaq- (all the faith went to all of the disbelief, my Lord, if You want not to be worshipped then it shall be), meaning that if Ali was killed then the disbelievers shall dare to kill me and kill all the muslims, and thus there shall be no faith and no Islam. Also he (PUH) said (the strike of Ali at the day of Khandaq is better than the worshipping of the two created [meaning human, and djinn])[1], so it is rightful to say that Islam is Mohammedan in existence... and Alawite in lasting, and thanks be to God and to Ali for the lasting of Islam!

`Abbási: let's suppose that your talk about `Umar and that he did change and take the caliphate by force is true, but why do you hate Abu-Bakr?

`Alawi: we hate him for many reasons and I shall mention two: first: for what he did to Fatima the daughter of the prophet (PUH) second: for not applying the law over the criminal and adulterer: Khalid ben Al-Waleed.

The king (surprised): and is Khalid ben Al-Waleed a criminal?

---

[1] Al-Fakhr Al-Rázi in Niháyat Al-`Uqool page104, Mustadrak Al-Hákim part 3, page32, Táreekh Baghdád part 3, page19, Al-Đahabi in Talkhees Al-Mustadrak part 3, page32, Arjah Al-Matálib page481.

`Alawi: yes.

The king: and what is his crime?

`Alawi: his crime is: Abu-Bakr sent him to the great companion Málik ben Nuwayrah -the one who the prophet (PUH) told him that he shall be in paradise- and he (Abu-Bakr) ordered hi (Khalid) to kill Málik and his people, and Málik was out of Medina, so when he saw Khalid coming to him with a small army, Málik commanded his people to carry the weapons, and so they did, and when Khalid reached them he tricked them and lied and swore to them by God that he is not going to harm them, and said to them: we are not here to fight you but we are guests for tonight, and so Málik got relaxed -because Khalid swore- and he put down the weapons with his people, and when it was the time to pray and Málik with his people stood up to pray they were attacked by Khalid and his army and got them tied and then killed them all, and then Khalid got greedy for the wife of Málik (when he saw that she's beautiful) and he raped her in the same night in which he killed her husband, and he made the head of her husband and his people as stones for the kettle to cook the food of his crime and ate with his army! and when Khalid got back to Medina, `Umar wanted to apply the law against him for killing muslims and for raping the wife of Málik, but Abu-Bakr (the believer!) denied that extremely, and by his deed he let go of the blood of the muslims and stopped a law of God!

The king (to the vizier): is it true what `Alawi said about Khalid and Abu-Bakr?

Vizier: yes this is what historians said![1]

The king: then why some people call Khalid as "the raised sword of God" ?

`Alawi: it is the paralyzed sword of the devil, but since he was an enemy for Ali ben Abi Tálib and was with `Umar in burning the door of the house of Fatima, some sunnis called him the sword of God!

The king: and are sunnis enemies for Ali ben Abi Tálib?

`Alawi: if they are not then why did they praise the one who took the caliphate by force from him and gathered around his enemies and denied his virtues, to the limit that they claim that Abu-Tálib [the father of Imam Ali] died as a disbeliever, while the truth is that Abu-Tálib was a believer and he pushed Islam further in the darkest days and protected the prophet in his calling [to Islam]!

The king: did Abu-Tálib turn into Islam?

`Alawi: Abu-Tálib was not a disbeliever to become a muslim, but he was... a faithful man that was hiding his faith, and when the prophet (PUH) was sent, Abu-Tálib showed his Islam and became the third muslim: the first was Ali ben Abi Tálib, the second was lady Khadeejah the wife of the prophet, and the third was Abu Tálib (PUH).

---

[1] of them: Abu Al-Fidá' in his history part 1, page158, and Al-Tabari in his history part 3, page241, and Ibn Al-Atheer in his history part 3, page149, and Ibn `Asákir in his history part 5, page105, and Ibn Katheer part 6, page321, and others.

The king (to the vizier): is it true what `Alawi is saying about Abu-Tálib?

Vizier: yes, some historians mentioned that[1].

The king: then why it is famous among sunnis that Abu-Tálib died as a disbeliever?

`Alawi: because Abu-Tálib is the father of imam Ali, the prince of the believers, so the envy of sunnis for Ali ben Abi Tálib (PUH) made them say that his father died as a disbeliever, as well as their envy also made them kill his two sons (Ali's) Al-Hasan and Al-Husayn, the masters of youth of paradise, so much that even sunnis that attended Karbala to kill Al-Husayn said: we fight you for our hate to your father and for what he did to our ancestors in the day of Badr and Hunayn!

The king (to the vizier): did the killers of Al-Husayn say this to Al-Husayn?

Vizier: historians mentioned that they said that to Al-Husayn!

The king (to `Abbási): and what is your answer about the story of Khalid ben Al-Waleed?

`Abbási: Abu-Bakr sought the (general) benefit from that!

`Alawi (surprised): sanctified is God! and what is that benefit that allows Khalid to kill the innocents and rape their women and then remain without a punishment, and even get the

---

[1] Al-Hákim fil-Mustadrak part 2, page623, Sharh Ibn Abi Al-Hadeed part 3, page313, and Táreekh Ibn Katheer part 3, page87, and Sharh Al-Bukhári for Al-Qastalani part 2, page227, and Al-Seerah Al-Halabiyyah part 1, page125, and lot of others. (the publisher)

leadership of the army, and Abu-Bakr says about him: he is a sword that God raised, so does the sword of God kills the disbelievers or the believers? and does the sword of God save the honor of muslims or rape the women of muslims??

`Abbási: suppose - O `Alawi - that Abu-Bakr made a mistake, but `Umar saved the situation!

`Alawi: saving the situation is by scourging Khalid for raping, and killing him for killing innocent believers, and `Umar did not do that, so `Umar made a mistake like Abu-Bakr did before.

The king: you `Alawi said in the beginning that Abu-Bakr... hurt Fatima the daughter of the prophet (PUH) so what did he do?

`Alawi: when Abu-Bakr made himself a ruler by force and terror, he sent `Umar and Qunfuð and Khalid ben Al-Waleed and Abu-`Ubaydah Al-Jarráh and some others - from the hypocrites - to the house of Fatima and Ali (PUT) and `Umar gathered the wood on the door of Fatima (that door that many times the prophet stood in front of it and said: Peace upon you O Household of prophecy, and didn't get inside unless he asked for permission) and he burnt the door with fire, and when Fatima came behind the door to stop `Umar from doing this with his followers, he squeezed her between the wall and the door so hard that she had abortion and a nail from the door planted in her chest and Fatima screamed: O father, O messenger of God, look what happened to us after you from Ibn Al-Khattáb [meaning `Umar] and Ibn Abi-Quháfah [meaning Abu-Bakr]! `Umar then looked around him and said: beat Fatima, so the lashes came down on the beloved of the prophet (PUH) until the blood gushed out from her body! And the effects of this squeeze and this shock remained drilling in the body of Fatima, and she became sick and sad until she left this life after her father within some days -

thus, Fatima is the martyr of the Household of the prophecy, and Fatima was killed... because of `Umar ben Al-Khattáb!

The king (to the vizier): is what `Alawi saying true?

Vizier: yes, I saw in some history books what the `Alawi is talking about![1]

`Alawi: and that's why shiites hate Abu-Bakr and `Umar!

`Alawi added: and the clue that this crime did happen by the hands of Abu-Bakr and `Umar, is that historians mentioned that Fatima died and she was angry at Abu-Bakr and `Umar and the prophet (PUH) mentioned in many occasions the hadith (God is satisfied for the satisfaction of Fatima and angry for her anger) and you O king know exactly what happens to someone that gets the wrath of God!?

The king (to he vizier): is that hadith true? and is it true that Fatima died and she was angry at Abu-Bakr and `Umar?

Vizier: yes, that was mentioned by scholars of Hadith and history![2]

`Alawi: and the clue for my argument: is that Fatima told Ali ben Abi Tálib (PUH) to not let Abu-Bakr and `Umar and the rest of

---

[1] Kitáb Al-Saqeefah for Abu-Bakr Al-Jawhari and Al-Imámah wal-Siyásah for Ibn Qutaybah, and Ibn Abi Al-Hadeed in Sharh Nahj Al-Balaghah part 2, page19. (the publisher)

[2] Saheeh Al-Bukhári, kitáb Al-Khums, hadith #2. In it also in the section of Khaybar invasion and in Kitáb Al-Fará'idh, and Saheeh Al-Tirmiði part 1, section of what is left of the inheritance of the prophet of God. Mustadrak Al-Saheehayn part 3, page153. Meezán Al-I`tidál part 2, page72. Kanz Al-`Ummál part 6, page219, and others. (the publisher)

those who wronged her attend her funeral, so they don't pray upon her, and never attend her burial, and to hide her tomb so that they don't attend to her grave, and imam Ali (PUH) did exactly what she asked for!

The king: this is weird, was such a thing done by Ali and Fatima?

Vizier: so was mentioned by historians!

`Alawi: also, Abu-bakr and `Umar hurt Fatima in another way!

`Abbási: and what is that?

`Alawi: they took the land of Fadak by force.

`Abbási: what is the clue that they took it by force?

`Alawi: the books of history mentioned that the prophet of God (PUH) gave Fadak to Fatima[1] so Fadak was in her hand -at the days of the prophet- and when the prophet died, Abu-Bakr and `Umar sent people to deport the workers of Fatima from Fadak by the sword and the force, and Fatima protested against Abu-Bakr and `Umar but they didn't listen to her, and even restrained her, and for this she never talked to them until she died with anger on them!

`Abbási: but `Umar ben `Abdul `Aziz [an umayyad ruler, almost ruled from 717AD-720AD] turned Fadak back to the children of Fatima -during his reign-?

`Alawi: and what is the use of that? If someone took your home by force and made you astray and then another man came after

---

[1] Fadak is a name for a land between Medina and Khaybar and it was owned by the prophet and he gave it to his daughter Fatima (PUH).

you die and gave back the home to your children, does that clear out the sin of the first aggressor?

The king: it is apparent from your speech you two - `Abbási and `Alawi - that you agree that Abu-Bakr and `Umar took by force the land of Fadak?

`Abbási: yes, history mentioned that[1].

The king: and why did they do so?

`Alawi: because they wanted to take the caliphate by force, and they knew that Fadak if it was to remain in the hands of Fatima then its production will be distributed (120,000 golden dinars as mentioned by some historians) among the people, and in that way people will gather around Ali (PUH), and this is what Abu-Bakr and `Umar hate!

The king: if these sayings are true then how strange is the situation of those! And if the leadership of these three was false, then who is the successor of the prophet (PUH)?

`Alawi: the prophet himself -and by a command from God- assigned the successors after him, in the hadith that is mentioned in the books of hadith when he said (my successors after me are twelve, as much as the tribes of the Israelites and all of them from Quraysh) [Quraysh: the name of the tribe of the prophet (PUH)].

The king (to the vizier): is it true that the prophet said that?

---

[1] Al-Haythami in his book part 9, page39. Al-Imámah wal-Siyásah and Sharh Nahj Al-Balaghah for Ibn Abi Al-Hadeed and others. (the publisher)

Vizier: yes.

The king: then who are these twelve?

`Abbási: four of them are known and they are: Abu-Bakr, `Umar, `Uthmán and Ali.

The king: and the rest?

`Abbási: there is a debate between the ulema.

The king: tell me their names.

`Abbási went silent.

`Alawi: O king, I shall mention their names for you as it was told in the books of sunnis, and they are: Ali, Al-Hasan, Al-Husayn, Ali, Muhammad, Ja`far (Jafar), Musa, Ali, Muhammad, Ali, Al-Hasan, Al-Mahdi (PUT)[1].

`Abbási: listen O king: shiites say that Al-Mahdi is alive since 255AH, and is that possible [this story happened in 485AH]? And they say: he will re-appear at the end of time to fill earth with justice after it had been full of unjust.

The king (to `Alawi): is it true you believe in that?

---

[1] 20 hadith from the prophet (PUH) were mentioned with the names of the twelve successors, by the way of sunni books, some of them: Fawá'id Al-Simtayn part 4. Taðkirat Ibn Al-Jawzi page378, Yanabee` Al-Mawaddah page442, Al-Arba`een for Al-Háfidh Abu Muhammad ben Abi Al-Fawáris, Maqtal Al-Husayn for Abi Al-Mu'ayyad, Mineháj Al-Fadhileen page239, Durar Al-Simtayn, and others. (the publisher)

`Alawi: yes that is true, because the prophet said that and it is mentioned by narrators of both shiites and sunnis.

The king: and how is it possible for a man to stay alive all that long time?

`Alawi: for now, not a thousand year did pass even from the age of Al-Mahdi [of course according to that time], and God says in Quran about the prophet Noah (and he continued with them for a thousand years save fifty years, 29:14), so is God unable to make someone live that long? Isn't God responsible for death and life and He is the Able over everything? then the prophet said that and he is true and believed in.

The king (to the vizier): is it true that the prophet foretold about Al-Mahdi like `Alawi said?

Vizier: yes [1]

The king (to `Abbási): then why do you deny the facts that was mentioned by us sunnis?

`Abbási: because I'm afraid over the creed of the public to be shaken up and their hearts might incline towards the shiites!

`Alawi: then you `Abbási are an example for God's saying (Lo! Those who hide the proofs and the guidance which We revealed, after We had made it clear to mankind in the Scripture: such are accursed of Allah and accursed of those who have the power to curse, 2:159) so you are included in the curse

---

[1] many sources for that, like: Al-Maláhim Wal-Fitan, section 19. `Aqd Al-Durar, hadith #26. Yanabee` Al-Mawaddah page491. Taðkirat Al-Khawás section 6. Hilyat Al-Awliyá'. Arjah Al-Matálib page378. Ðakhá'ir Al-`Uqbá for Al-Sháfi`i.

of God. then `Alawi said: O king, ask this `Abbási: should the scholar... keep the save the book of God and the sayings of the prophet of God, or should he save the creed of the public that is astraying from the book and sunna?

`Abbási: I save the creed of the public so that they don't incline toward the shiites because shiites are people of innovation!

`Alawi: the respected books tell us that your imam (`Umar) was the first one to make an innovation in Islam and he declared that himself when he said (what a good innovation is this) and that was in the story of the prayer of Taráweeh [Taráweeh: a long prayer done during Ramadan by sunnis in groups after the last prayer at night] when he ordered people to pray the Nafilah [Nafilah: a type of prayer in Islam that is not part of the five daily prayers but prayed as a donation] in groups, while God and the prophet prohibited praying a Nafilah in groups, so the innovation of `Umar was an obvious disobedience for God and the prophet![1] Then, did not `Umar make an innovation in the Aðán [Aðán: the call to pray] when he dropped (Come to the best of works) and added (prayer is better than sleeping)?[2] did

---

[1] Saheeh Al-Bukhári, section of Taráweeh prayer, Al-Sawá`iq, and Al-Qastaláni said in the book of Irshád Al-Sári fi Sharh Saheeh Al-Bukhári part 5, page4, when he reached `Umar saying (what a good innovation is this): he called it an innovation because the prophet of God did not assign it and it was not there at the time of Abu-Bakr and it was not at the beginning of the night and not in that much [meaning not that much rak`as, or the number of bows done by the prayer while he prays]. I say: yes, the caliph of muslims (!) innovate in religion - congratulations -.

[2] Al-Qawshaji mentioned and he is one of the greatest sunni ulema that `Umar said: three were at the time of the prophet and I ban them and punish for them: Mut`ah marriage, and Hajj Al-Tamattu` and (come to the best of works), and imam Málik [a sunni scholar who established a sub-school] said in Al-Mawte' that he got tidings saying

not he innovate when he canceled the share of non-muslims in opposition to God and His prophet? did not he innovate in banning Hajj Al-Tamattu` in opposition to God and His prophet? did not he innovate in banning Mut`ah marriage in opposition to God and His prophet? did not he innovate in not applying the law over the criminal and adulterer: Khalid ben Al-Waleed, in opposition to the command of God and His prophet about applying the law against the adulterer and the murderer? and so on with your innovations sunnis who follow `Umar. So, are you the people of innovation or is it us shiites?

The king (to the vizier): is it true what `Alawi mentioned about the innovations of `Umar in religion?

Vizier: yes, some ulema mentioned that in their books!

The king: then how do we follow someone that innovated in religion?

`Alawi: for this reason, following a person like that is a taboo, because the prophet (PUH) said (every innovation is a misguide, and every misguide is in hell), so the people who follow `Umar in his innovations - and they know about it - they are - surely - people of hell!

`Abbási: but the imams of the (islamic) schools (creeds) admitted the deed of `Umar?

---

that the caller for the pray came to `Umar ben Al-Khattáb to tell him that morning prayer is up and he found him asleep, so he said to him: praying is better than sleeping, so `Umar ordered him to make it part of the call to the morning prayer! I say: oh my God, is `Umar allowed to add and drop from the call to the prayer -which is a part of the religion- by his own desires and thought? (the publisher)

`Alawi: this is another innovation O king!

The king: and how is that?

`Alawi: because those who established these schools and they are: Abu Haneefah, Málik ben Anas, Al-Sháfi`i, and Ahmad ben Hanbal were not at the time of the prophet (PUH), but they came after him by almost 200 years, so were the muslims in that time between the prophet and those people all misguided? and what is the necessity of gathering all the creeds and ways in these four only and neglecting others? did the prophet advise so?

The king: what do you say `Abbási?

`Abbási: those were more wise than others!

The king: were there no wise man except of those?

`Abbási: but shiites also follow the creed of Ja`far Al-Sádiq [Jafar Al-Sádiq: the 6th imam for twelve shiites]?

`Alawi: we follow the school of Jafar because his way is the way of the prophet of God, because he is one of the Household whom God said about them (Allah's wish is but to remove uncleanness far from you, O Folk of the Household, and cleanse you with a thorough cleansing, 33:33), otherwise we follow all the twelve imams but since imam Jafar Al-Sádiq (PUH) was able to spread the knowledge and the interpretations and the holy hadiths more than other imams (because of some of the freedom at his time), and even 4000 pupils used to attend his school[1], and even he was able to renew the structure of Islam

---

[1] Al-Imám Al-Sádiq wal-Maðáhib Al-Arba`ah, Táreekh Baghdád, and others.

after the trials of umayyads and abbasids to erase it, thus for this shiites were called "jafarites" [or Ja`fari] according to the one who restored the structure of the creed and that is imam Jafar Al-Sádiq (PUH).

The king: what is your answer O `Abbási?

`Abbási: following the 4 schools is a habit for us sunnis!

`Alawi: you were but forced by some rulers, and you followed them like blind people without a clue!

`Abbási went silent.

`Alawi: O king, I testify that `Abbási shall be in hell if he remained like that.

The king: and how did you know that he shall be in hell?

`Alawi: because it is mentioned by the prophet (PUH) that he said (he who died and did not know the imam of his time, he shall die like an ignorant), so ask O king, who is the imam of `Abbási's time?

`Abbási: this hadith was not reported for the prophet.

The king (to the vizier): was this hadith reported or not?

Vizier: yes it was![1]

---

[1] sources: Al-Háfidh Al-Naysáboori in his Saheeh part 8, page108. Yanabee` Al-Mawaddah page117. Nafahát Al-Láhoot page3. Saheeh Muslim, and others.

The king (with anger): I thought you `Abbási are worthy for my trust but I've found out you are but a liar!

`Abbási: I know the imam of my time!

`Alawi: and who is he?

`Abbási: the king!

`Alawi: you should know O king that he is lying, and he is saying that to get closer to you!

The king: yes, I know he is lying, and I know myself that I cannot be the imam of time for the people, because I don't know anything, and I spend most of my time in hunting and in managing affairs! then said the king: O `Alawi, then who do you think is the imam of time?

`Alawi: the imam of time in my creed is imam Al-Mahdi (PUH) as we talked about him before as reported from the prophet (PUH), and whoever knew him shall die as a muslim and he is in paradise, and he who didn't know him died as an ignorant and he shall be in hell with the people of ignorance!

Here, the face of the king shined, and the signs of happiness appeared on his face and looked upon the attendance and said: you should know O people, that I'm satisfied with this debate (which lasted for three days) and I am sure now that the truth is with shiites in everything they say and believe in, and the sunnis are people of a false creed and an astraying belief, and I am one man that when recognizes the truth, shall obey it and admit it, and I shall not be a man of falsehood in this life and a man of hell in the Hereafter. For this, I announce in front of you that I've become a shiite, and who loves to be with me let him follow me and be a shiite, by the blessings of God and His mercy, and let himself be out from the darkness of the falsehood to the light of the truth!

Vizier: and I knew that, and shiites are right, and that the right school is the shiites' only. I knew that since I was a pupil, and for this I announce that I am too a shiite.

Thus, most of the ulema and the ministers and the generals who attended in the court (and they counted almost as 70) got into the creed of shiites.

The tidings of the turning of the king and the vizier Nizam Al-Mulk and the ministers and the generals and the writers into shiites, reached all the lands, and many people got into the creed of shiites, and Nizam Al-Mulk ordered - and he is the father of my wife - that teachers should teach the creed of shiites in Nizamiyyah schools in Baghdad!

But some sunni ulema that insisted on the falsehood remained on their creed like God said (became as rocks, or worse than rocks, for hardness, 2:74).

And they started to plot against the king and Nizam Al-Mulk and blamed him for that because he was the planning mind for the land, until the dirty hand got him -by the orders of those stubborn sunnis- and they assassinated him in the 12th of Ramadan, year 485AH, and after that they assassinated Malikshah Saljuqi (Malikshah I). we are to God and we shall get back to Him. They were killed on the way of God and for the truth and faith, so congratulations for them and for everyone that gets killed on the way of God and for the truth and the faith. and I made a poem of lamentation for the great sheikh Nizam Al-Mulk and this is some of it: the vizier Nizam Al-Mulk was a pearl so dear made by the merciful from honor so dear and days did not know its value so He for jealousy turned it back to the shell he chose the creed of right in a debate that showed the truth in an obvious clue the creed of shiites is a truth with no false and everything else is just a mirage with a false portiere but a deep envy they moved for him and the full moon of the night remained in an eclipsed shade upon him shall be a thousand peace from God that follow that are read over his soul in the eternity and the houses (of paradise)

That, and I was an attendant in the court and the debate, and I've recorded everything that happened in the court, but I've canceled additions, and made the story short in this book.

And thank be to God alone, and peace be upon Muhammad and his good Household and his true followers.

I wrote it in Baghdad in Nizamiyyah school.

Muqátil ben `Atiyyah

www.ingramcontent.com/pod-product-compliance
Lightning Source LLC
Chambersburg PA
CBHW051553010526
44118CB00022B/2695